a BEACON of Light

For more information, contact:
Fig Factor Media, LLC | www.figfactormedia.com

Cover Design by DG Marco Alvarez
Layout by LDG Juan Manuel Serna Rosales

Printed in the United States of America

ISBN: 978-1-957058-98-6
Library of Congress Control Number: 2022923436

FIG
FACTOR
MEDIA

a BEACON of Light

ESCAPING THE DARKNESS OF FINANCIAL ABUSE

LORAINE GARCIA-GODFREY, MPA

To all those suffering in silence from the wounds of abusive relationships. Society should not treat domestic violence as a taboo subject. It needs to be brought out into the light for change to occur. Nothing good happens in darkness. Everyone knows someone, whether they realize it or not, who is experiencing abuse. Please treat them with love, kindness, and help them stand up against domestic violence.

Light has come into the world…Everyone who does evil hates the light, and will not come into the light for fear that their deeds will be exposed. But whoever lives by the truth comes into the light, so that it may be seen plainly that what they have done has been done in the sight of God.

-John 3:19-21, NIV

TABLE OF CONTENTS

ACKNOWLEDGEMENTS

First, I am grateful to God for gifting me with my mission as a warrior for those who are in need, especially women and children hurting from domestic violence. I would not change it for the world. I am prepared and armored up for the battles ahead. My passion for this work is immeasurable and I realize it is a blessing to know my purpose.

Second, I am thankful for my two beautiful and resilient children, Alexa, and Sean. They continue to amaze me with their kindness and strength of character. I look forward to watching them continue to thrive throughout their lives.

I would like to thank my husband, Greg, for loving me in the way I need to be loved; to allow me to use my gifts to flourish. I no longer feel stifled, I am happy to be my authentic self, and I am grateful for that.

Finally, I want to thank my parents for always supporting me 110% in everything. I know it is a very special gift to receive steadfast, unwavering, and lifelong encouragement. They are responsible for teaching me to believe in non-judgmental and unconditional love for others.

INTRODUCTION

The first step to leaving an abusive relationship is realizing you are in one, which can be very difficult to identify and even admit to oneself when there is so much confusion and chaos purposely added to the relationship by the abuser. But once you do, what comes next?

Ninety-nine percent of domestic violence relationships include some sort of financial abuse, whether it is taking control of your money or controlling what you get to spend. This type of abuse can damage a person's economic status significantly, as well as their mental and physical health. From identifying the different types of abuse to providing resources and ways to escape your situation, reading this book is your first move towards reaching your safe haven and stepping out of the darkness of financial abuse.

Leaving is not easy, but everyone deserves to live in peace and safety. It is time to step out of the darkness and find your beacon of light.

PART 1

a SPARK of Light

TYPES OF RELATIONSHIP ABUSE

Relationship abuse is sometimes called domestic violence, domestic abuse, or intimate partner abuse. Experiencing relationship abuse is very damaging and can come from a spouse, or other intimate partner, a parent, a child, an employer, or anyone else with whom there is a relationship.

The goal of a domestic violence offender is to gain power and control over their target. Controlling behavior is a tactic for the abuser to maintain dominance over the victim. The abuser believes that they are justified in the controlling behavior and often the victim may go along at first to keep the peace, but slowly the controlling behavior grows to the point that it stifles them causing harm.

HERE ARE SOME COMMON FORMS OF ABUSE: *

Emotional/Verbal Abuse

Non-physical behavior, such as threats, insults, screaming, constant monitoring, isolation, or silent treatment.

Stalking

Being repeatedly watched, followed, monitored, or harassed. Occurs online or in person and can include giving unwanted gifts.

Physical Abuse

Any intentional use of physical touch to cause fear, injury, or assert control, such as hitting, shoving, spitting, and strangling.

Digital Abuse

Using technology to bully, stalk, threaten, or intimidate a partner by using texting, social media, apps, or other electronic tracking.

Sexual Abuse

Any sexual activity that occurs without willing, active, unimpaired consent, such as unwanted sexual touch, sexual assault (rape), and tampering with contraceptives.

Spiritual Abuse

Misusing spiritual authority to control the partner. Taking scripture out of context to inflict further abuse and to use power over partners.

Post-Separation Abuse

Using the courts to wield power over their partner through vexatious litigation and using child custody as a bargaining chip. Refusing to co-parent, but instead practices counter-parenting.

Financial Abuse (Sometimes Called Economic Abuse)

Taking complete control over all finances, including blocking their partner from earning money independently and/or ruining their credit.

*https://www.breakthecycle.org

WHAT IS FINANCIAL ABUSE?

Domestic violence is a broad term that encompasses many areas of cruel mistreatment. As discussed, the different types include physical, emotional, verbal, psychological, financial, digital, spiritual, and post-separation abuse. It is important to note that all types, not just physical harm, still fall under the category of "domestic violence." This book will focus on financial or economic abuse.

Financial abuse is when someone takes control of your money or stops you from being financially independent by earning your own money. Economic abuse is extremely common in situations of domestic abuse, occurring in 99 percent of all cases.* This type of abuse can significantly, or completely, destroy a person's economic status. It is difficult, but not impossible, to recover. Examples of financial abuse will be covered in this book, as well as some action steps to take to repair your credit and to improve, or even to restore, your finances. Financial abuse is very often one of the top reasons many people do not leave an abusive intimate partner. Sometimes it may be the only reason. Also, it can be a top reason someone returns to an abusive intimate partner. Unfortunately, the statistics reveal that between 21 percent to 60 percent of victims of violence from intimate partners lose their jobs directly due to the domestic abuse they experience.

---

* NCADV, Quick Guide: Economic and Financial Abuse. 2017. https://ncadv.org/blog/posts/quick-guide-economic-and-financial-abuse#:~:text=Between%2094%2D99%25%20of%20domestic,reasons%20stemming%20from%20the%20abuse

FORMS OF FINANCIAL ABUSE

Financial Abuse comes in many forms, such as:

- Controlling your money, for example, by overseeing all the household income and paying you an allowance.

- Controlling how all the household income is spent.

- Keeping you from working or making your own money or by sabotaging your job.

- Impairing your ability to attend school.

- Forcing you to work in a family business without being paid.

- Filing fraudulent insurance claims.

- Forcing you to claim Social Security benefits.

- Making you sign as a guarantor on a loan or taking a loan out in your name.

- Forcing you to open a credit card for their use and/or to damage your credit.

Financial abuse can be present with other forms of abuse, like physical or emotional abuse, but also can be present without these other behaviors. Sometimes financial abuse can seem like a demonstration of affection initially, like your partner offering to take control of the finances to take the pressure off you. In some cases, it can be an attempt to control your access to money.

SIGNS OF FINANCIAL ABUSE

It is important to know the signs of financial abuse. Abusers use finances to control their partners and to keep them in the relationship. Just like other forms of abuse, it is very powerful. It often begins subtly and progresses over time. The goal of the abuser is to make their partner increasingly more financially dependent on them to maintain control over them.

There are many different warning signs of financial abuse occurring in a relationship. Not being allowed to earn money on your own is a sign you are experiencing financial abuse, as well as taking it from you if you do earn it. Another example is checking the mileage on the odometer after you use the car. There may be several little hints that all add up to the fact you are being victimized in this way.

Financial abuse can occur throughout a relationship, or may begin after you and your partner have split up, for example, by hiding assets or withholding child support. A domestic abuse survivor shared how her abusive husband hid income during their divorce trial, claiming his salary decreased by $200,000 the year the divorce began. He owned his own business and it is very uncommon for accounting firms to lose that much business so arbitrarily. The judge did not require any further proof, so using his "new" income as a basis for the distribution of assets the judge did not allow any alimony for the survivor. She had stayed home to raise their children for over 12 years while helping him build his business. A couple of weeks after the divorce was finalized, he purchased a house entirely with cash. It became clear he had hidden money he received as payment from clients to ensure she would not receive a fair settlement. In fact, he told her he wanted to destroy her and would ensure that she would leave with nothing. Because he was losing control of her, he wished to inflict as much damage as he could.

COMMON ABUSE TACTICS

Some common tactics that abusers use to control your finances include the following:

- Stopping you from getting a job or from working at a job you have.

- Stopping you from going to work or attending important meetings by keeping you up all night or physically hurting you.

- Stopping you from studying.

- Giving you an "allowance."

- Refusing to pay bills for accounts that are in your name to ruin your credit.

- Forcing you to turn over your paychecks or public benefit checks.

- Forcing you to account for all the money you spend by showing receipts.

Limiting your access to money is also a method of abuse. Examples include:

- Not giving you access to bank accounts.

- Denying you access to money so you cannot buy basic needs, like food or medicine.

- Destroying, damaging, or stealing your property.

- Racking up debt on shared accounts or credit cards.

- Withholding financial support, like child support payments.

- Refusing to work or to contribute anything to the household income.

- Gambling away your money or shared money.

- Hiding assets from you.

LEAVING IS NOT EASY

Usually there are several types of abuse going on in an abusive relationship. There may be a combination of any of these types of abuse, psychological, spiritual, sexual, physical, intimidation, isolation, emotional, stalking, verbal (coercion, threats, and blame), using male privilege, and financial or economic abuse. I have met many women who are considering leaving their abuser but they cannot because they either are not making enough money or they have no income at all. This is the number one reason most women cannot leave abusive relationships.

Many women have difficulty seeing that they are, indeed, in a financially abusive relationship. This is usually due to the insidious nature of this abuse. It occurs slowly, over time, and incrementally so that a victim may not realize what exactly is happening. It is also common for a victim to feel too embarrassed to discuss their situation with someone else. That is true of all the types of abuse.

The reasons why some women stay in financially abusive relationships can be because they believe that they do not have enough money to manage on their own, they do not have anywhere to go, they fear for their children's financial security, or they lack confidence in their ability to support themselves and/or their children.

For those who have never experienced this, one must understand that living in abusive relationships wears down a person's self-confidence, self-worth, and belief in their own abilities. This negatively alters their very foundation.

A Survivor's Story

"Over several years, I slipped into the role of a financial abuse victim—without even noticing. Starting out as equals, our marriage changed drastically after we started a family. I was strongly discouraged from working outside the home. Although I loved being home with my babies, later when I was ready to go back to work, I was put-down for even bringing up the topic. By preventing me from working he had all the control in the relationship. He slowly convinced me that I was not worth as much as he was. That sounds so crazy, but I could not see clearly at the time. I had lost all my self-esteem and confidence and was merely a shell of the woman I used to be, because of all the emotional and psychological abuse I suffered. Of course, he had a completely different persona to the outside world, where he was a successful businessman and a community leader. Everyone always said, 'He's such a nice guy.' I finally came to realize that I was under his complete control.

He dragged out the divorce proceedings for years, and stopped paying the mortgage while living in the marital home. It took three years for the bank to foreclose on our house. He did this on purpose because my name was on the mortgage as well as his. It was his goal to ruin my credit and he was successful. He did not care about his credit because he was receiving enough cash to buy whatever he wanted.

Looking back, I am now fully aware of just how the financial abuse occurred. It took me a long time to get my life back, and I hope by talking to other women about the signs, they can pull themselves out or not even get into this situation to begin with."

—Leah*, a survivor

*Name has been changed

PART 2

OUT OF *the Dark*

HOW TO IDENTIFY IF YOU ARE BEING FINANCIALLY ABUSED

Financial abuse happens slowly.

Just like all forms of domestic violence, financial abuse does not start immediately in a relationship. Abusers do not show their true colors in the very beginning of relationships. If they did, their new partner would not stay with them. Domestic abuse is insidious in the way it creeps into a relationship. In cases where abuse does start early in the relationship, the victim may think there was an isolated incident or that she may be able to change his behavior.

Financial abuse is a concealed abuse that does not begin until the relationship is a committed one, when the abuser starts forming a "trauma bond" with their partner. The abusive cycle begins and the abuser tries to breach their partner's strengths. Contrary to what many people believe, abusers target someone with a lot of strengths—not someone they would consider to be weak or an easy target. The abuser seeks someone with strengths that make them feel good about being partnered with them. Then, the abuser pursues and appropriates those strengths they see in the other person by breaking them down psychologically.*

---

*Thomas, S. Exposing Financial Abuse: When Money Is a Weapon. (MAST Publishing House, 2018).

GET YOUR LIFE BACK

Okay, so you are now fully aware of how damaging financial abuse has been in your life. Remember, it is not your fault. If you have been in an abusive relationship, your abuser has chosen to mess with your head—and everything else—to make you unaware of all his or her insidious actions and intents. What can you do to take back your life? Here are some action steps:

- Believe in yourself.
- Find a job.
- Become financially educated.

According to Kristen Paruginog, founder, and executive director of Break the Silence Against Domestic Violence, the first thing needed is a mindset that you **can** do this. After leaving an abusive relationship, a survivor's self-esteem is shattered and it is up to them to get it back. So, believing in yourself is the first step.[*]

Next, you will need to find a job to support yourself financially, which can feel like a monumental undertaking if you have not worked outside the home in a long time. If you need help writing a resume, ask friends or family members for help. Many libraries, community colleges, large churches, etc. may offer assistance or free courses on resume-writing. You might need to be creative, especially if you have not worked before. Think about unique ways you might be able to earn some income, for example, if you are crafty, try selling your crafts online, or if you have another talent, such as cooking, singing, or playing a musical instrument, consider teaching others.

[*] Domesticshelters.org. "Finding your financial footing after abuse." 2017. https://www.domesticshelters.org/articles/financial/finding-your-financial-footing-after-abuse

The next step is important—you will need to become financially educated. You can take an online course; there are many free ones. You will need to learn how to create a budget and how to repair your credit. Then you can set financial goals to accomplish what you want to do next, like buy a car or pay for college. There are resources available to help with these steps you will need to take. The Allstate Foundation has a domestic violence program that has a stated mission of ending domestic violence through financial empowerment. On its website, you can find educational resources that provide tools to help domestic violence survivors recover from financial abuse.[*]

You should also reach out to a domestic violence advocate in your area. There are many programs in every state that could help you with local housing assistance, childcare programs, job placement, and financial education. If you need to find a local domestic violence organization and do not know where to start, you can always call the National Domestic Violence Hotline at (800) 799-SAFE (7233), or text START to the same hotline number, or go online to its website at https://www.thehotline.org.

---

[*] Allstate Foundation. 2021. https://allstatefoundation.org/what-we-do/end-domestic-violence/resources.

PROTECTING YOUR FINANCES BEFORE LEAVING

First, you will need to put aside small amounts of money over time to build an escape fund. You may consider asking a trusted friend or family member to look after the money for you or to assist you financially. Next, you will need to gather important financial documents or make copies of them. Include in this list: bank statements, checkbooks, title deeds, paystubs, credit card statements, car registration, tax returns, utility bills, and loan statements and mortgages. You also should procure any other important legal documents, such as birth certificates, passports, marriage certificates, immigration documents, Medicare or Medicaid cards, driver's license, will, prenuptial agreement, and any other court orders or documents. Keep them safely away from your home.

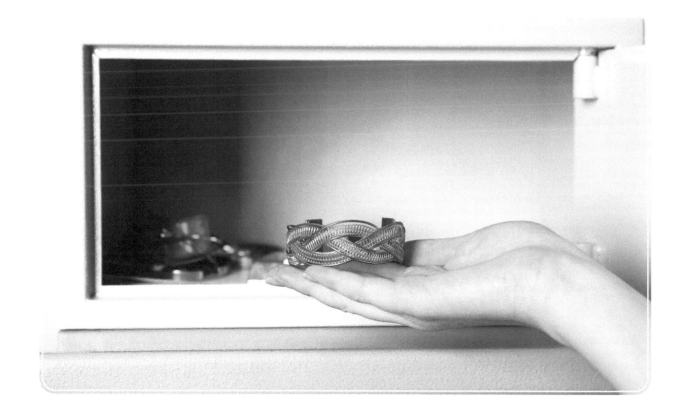

PROTECTING YOUR FINANCES AFTER LEAVING

Opening a bank account is the next important step. Then, deposit or transfer any monies you can into it. This must be done very carefully, because you need to ensure you can complete it safely. In addition, if you can obtain a safe deposit box at a bank you can store the important financial and legal documents previously mentioned in it as well as other valuables you wish to keep safe.

Your new bank account should be opened in your name only, not jointly. Regarding joint bank accounts and credit cards, you should withdraw money you need, freeze the account, inform the bank of your separation, cancel any direct deposits and debits. If your home mortgage has a line of credit, change the terms, so both signatures are needed to withdraw money.

It is important to change all your PINs, passwords, and security questions for your cell phone account, bank and credit card accounts, online shopping accounts, email, and social media accounts. If you and your partner use a banking app, make sure you unregister their device so they cannot access your personal bank account.

As far as your housing situation, if you are moving out of a rental, have your name removed from the lease. Obtain legal advice if you are living in a home owned by either one of you or both. You may be able to negotiate remaining in the family home. An attorney will be able to advise you on obtaining a protection order, if necessary. Also, many courthouses have some form of free or affordable court assistance, as well as in-court domestic violence services.

WHAT CAN YOU DO FOR YOURSELF?

What can you do for yourself? You can be EMPOWERED!

If, after reading this book, you recognize some, many, or all the manipulation tactics discussed here and recognize them as what you are experiencing, please take the necessary steps to heal yourself.

All types of domestic abuse can cause trauma. At Out of the Dark, we are committed to helping domestic violence survivors heal all aspects of their being: mind, body, and spirit. You can find more information on the complexities of domestic violence and the trauma informed care that Out of the Dark provides to survivors by going to our website at www.outofdark.org. Programs include support groups, court advocacy, spiritual support, lay counseling, financial education, and job search assistance. Out of the Dark also provides wellness coaching that addresses the proper nutritional needs of women in need of healing from trauma. Many women have had emotional breakthroughs by attending our group sessions. They regain strength, can see more clearly, and feel better about themselves, leading them to move on in their lives to better days. Community and support can do wonders for one's self-confidence.

Thank you for taking an important step in your healing journey by reading this book. To learn more about other types of domestic violence email help@outofdark.org.

MOVING FORWARD

It can certainly be overwhelming to consider all the things that need to be addressed and handled for you to gain control of your finances. Your mental health is something you need to care for and, it should be mentioned, you do not have to complete all these actions immediately. You can turn your attention to some of them after you have some breathing space.

Financial abuse often accompanies post-separation abuse. After one of the parties in a relationship ends or tries to end that relationship, the abuser uses finances as a weapon to "punish" the survivor. Post-separation abuse has formally been identified as another devastating device used by abusers.

Although this entire process can feel very long and painful, there is still so much hope for a better life ahead for you and your children! Remember, there are many resources available for women coming out of abusive relationships. Anyone experiencing abuse should know that they do not need to walk alone.

RESOURCES FOR HELP

- National Domestic Violence Hotline: (800) 799-SAFE (7233) for 24-hour support, or text START to the same hotline number, or https://www.thehotline.org

- Illinois Domestic Violence Helpline: (877) 863-6338.

- Illinois Coalition Against Violence: (217) 789-2830 or https://www.ilcadv.org

- DomesticShelters.org, an online resource for statewide and national hotlines, services, and articles for domestic violence victims: www.domesticshelters.org

- National Coalition Against Domestic Violence, provides services for domestic violence survivors, and advocates: www.ncadv.org

- Out of the Dark provides services and programs to help in healing from abuse and trauma: (630) 400-6512 or (630) 400-5402; help@outofdark.org or www.outofdark.org

AUTHOR BIO

Loraine Garcia-Godfrey is the co-founder of the nonprofit organization Out of the Dark which addresses domestic violence and helps those who need healing from all types of relationship abuse. She has spent over a decade volunteering as an advocate in this field while working full-time in the legal field. She earned her Master of Public Administration degree, but she is most proud of her two children and admires the cheerful and empathetic adults they have become. Her husband of four years is a pillar of strength for her as she spreads her wings for the first time in her professional life.